BRIGHT SPECIMEN

Bright Specimen

POEMS

Julie Poole

Deep Vellum Publishing
Dallas, Texas

Deep Vellum Publishing
3000 Commerce St., Dallas, Texas 75226
deepvellum.org · @deepvellum

Deep Vellum is a 501c3 nonprofit literary arts organization
founded in 2013 with the mission to bring
the world into conversation through literature.

Support for this publication has been provided in part by grants from the
National Endowment for the Arts, the Texas Commission on the Arts, the City
of Dallas Office of Arts and Culture's ArtsActivate program, and the Moody
Fund for the Arts:

ISBNs: 978-1-64605-057-4 (paperback) | 978-1-64605-058-1 (ebook)

LIBRARY OF CONGRESS CATALOGING IN PUBLICATION DATA

Names: Poole, Julie, 1980– author.
Title: Bright specimen : poems / Julie Poole.
Description: First edition. | Dallas, Texas : Deep Vellum Publishing, 2021.
Identifiers: LCCN 2020048014 (print) | LCCN 2020048015 (ebook) | ISBN
9781646050574 (trade paperback) | ISBN 9781646050581 (ebook)
Subjects: LCGFT: Poetry.
Classification: LCC PS3616.O63727 B75 2021 (print) | LCC PS3616.O63727
(ebook) | DDC 811/.6—dc23
LC record available at https://lccn.loc.gov/2020048014
LC ebook record available at https://lccn.loc.gov/2020048015

Cover design by Aileen Morrow | aileenmorrow.com

Interior Layout and Typesetting by KGT

Printed in the United States of America. The paper in this book contains 100%
post-consumer fiber and is manufactured via renewable energy and is chlorine-
free. The ink is a vegetable-based dye.

For Chaya

CONTENTS

the green earth / oxygen
  —Larry Eigner

Oh Sumptuous / moment / Slower go
  —Emily Dickinson

let me describe to you
a pasture mosaic
the last paragliders
have left and the sky
is a sheet of yellow
it's too late for birds
every animal's been fed
time takes on a tea-color
things have quieted down
waving flowers turn into shined brass
bobbing and waving
a hushed symphony
the dinner plates have been cleaned
we've put on our second sweaters
work is done piece by piece by piece
they don't have to match
this you realize quickly
one tile color suggests
another in order to make movement
curve this way
and the opposite
keep placing until all moves
in one direction
there's order in
a shy existence
beauty's a responsibility
it requires making a mess
there's room for all
shapes and patterns
the sun is a daily
teacher each hour
after 4:00 fades
and the emergent colors
tell a different
part of the story
Even as the sun
sets it keeps track
of you watches
you work
reminds you of
all the green
it's made
today

I am firm in my green idea
it slathers out from me
the pressure it took to apply
one thick stroke of saying
Green I dominate
A   giant spear of grass
fingers   raking down the page
I am powerful with my message
my entire body gets behind
the leaf

A tiger's stripes are warmed
to the sides of the tiger's body
that's how the colors become flush
under the heat of the sun
at two times of day
dawn and dusk

This color is a steady idea I cannot name
is it a blood stain
is it white
blushing tanned or jaundiced
Yellow   or day light
mummified skin
A   locust
The hour this color comes from
is early evening when
everything's blanketed in
Fall's glow   cold is approaching
Summer's made a mess
of me
&
now only the Greeks
can save
my ear

two green highways
some evening light
some early morning light
in the middle
two   green highways
a   confident brushstroke
dabs of triangular
paint
Don't tell me what to do
the message is
confident in the
beginning the middle
and   the end
such assuredness prevents
my delicate heads
from breaking
I've created my
body
I've created a
home for
expression
when I reach beyond
what I should
green is a decision
frail necks emerge
something is caught
in my
throat

simple   linens   sun
a   marbled heat that still allows
for conversations on things
other than the weather
She has a scent-message jasminum
every so often a new fragrant note plays
my senses say can this be happening?
My eyes are nearly watering from the smell
lavender was by these standards mute
the leaves are thin   folds of rubber
leather-textured olive green with a clean
crease down the center
in the blossom's middle
some protruding part
that   feels   nude-like
intimate   a sex-part
the center where the white paint
folds   out is a radical chip
broken along the end
paper mache
How   could I fold vanilla paper like this?
an origami of overlapping petals
fragrant sheets
it can be so good
to dream alone
in a hospital-house
with open windows
ice tea clinking
in a glass
pitcher
nothing's   a chore
when everything
you touch
a sweating glass
a warm sheet
has an easy
temperature

Rosa rugosa

I remember being a small fruit
my mother dressed me up like
a sock and covered my head
with a pointy hat we went out-
side and I saw my first
snow and my first green
shiny leaf I blinked
at the sun and sneezed
my first allergy to
light a big bright star
on fire the sensations
of being alive so strange
my neck was new
and I didn't know
How to bend it
I'd look up & how heavy
it was to work
the heavy thing
upright again
The first sound I want
to believe was
my mother through many
years the pitch of my voice
has grown to meet hers
almost identical
I don't remember my first
sense of dread
but I think of it
when ever I see
a baby cry

the landscape where they found
   Iris was a scar
a half-prairie the sun on
    the brink of setting
    the kingdom has collapsed
mud drifts and entire houses
    slide down a hillside
    I can't forget each summer
    fires raged   rain melted
   the rest of the destruction
    it was a cleared slate
    the fate of families
    smothered their breath
     snuffed out like a match
     had there been greenery to catch it
     had there been strongly wedded
      hills small townships whipped off
      preventable the sound of walls
      cracking twigs a sort of
        brown snow
        avalanche

Iris says my roots are
longer than my life
my leaves grew quickly
when I grew a head
I saw what I'd only
sensed happening all around
the briefest moment
a growth of eyes
and a tongue to taste
the atmosphere I too have
had a body longer
than a face through my
skin I breathed in
my mother's affection
the first element I
touched was liquid
I do not remember
seeing a bright light
I do not remember
pressure on my new
shoulders
or the first draft
of electrified air
perhaps the sensation
that registers most
is my chest and
stomach pressed
against warm breathing
like the swelling of waves
rising falling
a buoyant living
surface
to rest on

order lifts
its two wings
sound cracks out
like wet sheets
bells ring balance
is attained I believe
I have a purpose
let's suppose I tell
a story about flowers
how they first grew
and the human woman's
body mimicked them
her womb held life
right and left
all the curving shapes
combined into a supreme
goodness I never doubted
this capacity the scales of justice
carried in my simple body
I do believe I know right
from wrong in a room full of
women I am calm and light
suddenly it seems possible
no harm will come to anyone
the atmosphere is forgiving I've
managed to disappear into a day-
dream the noises in the back-
ground are just chatter the sort
you could comfortably sleep to

unable to have a child
    I named my dog Indigo
      she's a blue heeler aussie-shepherd mix
her tail's   been dipped in black paint
   she has an interior world
      I'm not always privy to
   it cracks me up how
     we're both passengers
       in the same way
     I like to watch
      the land roll by
       sometimes in utter silence
    as the sun comes up
     making me take off my sweater
without a husband I can feel other women
     silently asking me if I've ever
      felt loved   by a man no
       by the earth yes
    I guess it's all relative
    I got Indigo at 39
     when I relearned how to drive
    bought a truck
    and knew I'd be alone
    a lot on the road
     who's protecting who here I don't know
The world's a dangerous place
     I tell her
       she just pants which sounds
         to me like laughing

Castilleja purpurea

to New Mexico
in search of a color
I've never seen not sure
if it would be found
in a tapestry or the sky
or some rocky formation
not sure how the color
would make me feel
but I'd seen some
faintly familiar
tone on a paintbrush
specimen & that only affirmed
my instinct for vastness
a particular tint
like a particular sound
the color I was
sure could only
emerge out of
a great expanse
it would mark
itself across my chest
and make me stand
tall naturally
in seconds it would
be gone the
exact conditions
to replicate it
weather and
light would
change this was
all just a sense
I had like a piece of music
I had to hear but no name to look it up by

Nymphaea odorata

A hook with
a wedding dress
on the end
a diagram
for where to pin
a corsage
a signature
annulling the
marriage of a
god and a
mortal
the voice
of Lady
Day
the sheets
a young bride
wants
but won't
ask for
day-two
snow
when
sparrows
have drawn
maps
and it's still
too cold
for any other
animal
a piece
of
jewelry
wrapped
in tissue
too beautiful
to wear
a road
that was
lost
and a
road
that is
beginning
a new explanation
for how
babies
are born
the sort
of woman
I want
to
become

marsh grass sun
a dried out snake skin
root-colors teak
      strong as a knuckle bone
            thin leaves
              high pitched
      in the wind parched sounding
            the passes clear
      snow a distant
            feature blanketing
              everything round
            a river that won't
                  belong to any one
            state weaves
                  its solid body
                        through and out
                  again hooking its
                        giant arms
                        around tree stumps
                        and boulders
                        Lakes twinning
                        Lakes solid
                              and alone
                        various altitudes
                        various ways
                              of stretching
                              across the
                              familiar and
                                unknown

Iris tenuissima

A map of a network of streams
  is captured on an iris petal
    sheer and now colorless
    trickles of water can be heard
  circulating   rocks are wet and shining
        riverlets wedged in between release
    small noises bubbling Hemlock needles
  drop and spin on the surface of
            ice cold water
          the map has been duplicated
            again and again
          each element mimics another
        water moves like blood through a vein
        veins move through iris like water

Nelumbo lutea

underwater gardens
 umbrellas too big
 they have to fold
   tablecloths wet
       dresses where does
    the flower go does it sit
      on top a weird hat
          is it sheltered by
       a disc big as a vinyl record
          the music that spins out
            listen raindrops listen
             raindrops   on elephant
          skin proud lily
             proud mary
       the sound of a distant
                train woosh of
             parasols bobbing
                 surface mushrooms
              able to walk on water
                 plants able to walk on water
        what did you do today
              I ate two tacos
          and was moody
                It's winter no time
               for swimming last night
         the rain whooped and rattled my blinds
               scared me like an intruder
                    the sky's gone mad
              what have we done
              this time ? how
           many people are dead?
            each droplet a bleeding
               man each gust
               a woman found buried

through trout lily
I see an underwater shadow
a thick line
a bend of moon
still trying to grow
the petals lift
off the page
one reaches its
arm around its
stalk another
curls upwards
licks its lip
the shadows
I see are
milky
water
still trying
to ripple
through
leaves

Nymphaea mexicana

No the sun was
    born out of water
it died in the sky
  this process happens
    every day &
   we think our
      lives are short
     Nymphaea can't help
    but mimic all
      she sees
       by turning yellow
      by watching the
        moon she learns
        how to dance
          steps no one
            can replicate
        she waits for the opera
         singer standing
           in the boat
          to arrive
          she waits
         for each
           orchestra
       member to drift by
         on their leafy rafts
        never touching
         but the music does
         it rises and bumps
        and drifts
          frogs and salamanders
         surface to watch
        why do you
        think night's
        such an
       active time
       they're
      shouting
         encore encore

this green beetle's
　　story ended
in '92 when
　　the aquatic
　　lily was lifted
　　　from the Guadalupe
　　River and rolled
　　　　out like moist
　　dough the page
　　a sorry container
I'm sorry too
　　　Beetle
unless you've been
　　　bad naughty
　　eating your way
　　　　through destiny
　　　Oh my pretty
　　　　pin-pricked friend
　　　　　wearing your green
　　　　and gold disco
　　　clothes head
　　　and legs flattened
　　　by time
　　heading toward
　　　　the flower's
　　　　tunnel

Lilium michauxii

when your life gets too big
leaf and stem it's lopped off
the two parts halved
grow next to each other
this lily grew two pages
in length her beginning
to the left of her end
while the loud story
of her color is gone
what remains is still
talkative she's
dashing her form
seems impossible
I want to hook
her back
to see how she
stands & take
note this is how
you become limitless
6 parts each
contributing a first rate
anatomy
I have so much to learn
about how to carry my worth
& sense of prosperity

Lavandula vera

We are together
all wisps
listing out
what joyful dead
aroma a heat
a memory
in order to fit
a joint
is bent
the ending's where
the flowers happen
living they were
bluish
dead they are sage
still harboring
sunlight
in a vein
Lavandula vera
6 figures cannot
compare
Lavandula vera
my lovely
under magnification
a structure appears
a puppet fabric
sparkling
a soft-but-
not soft
glistening felt
spotted
"This is where the
scent pockets are"
the leaf that comes with it
is a leathery ear
fine hairs
and cracked
like a desert
crushed I notice
the small
yellow tubes
ridges of almonds
a grainy texture
Sea-music
somewhere

in california
I learned how to sculpt
took shapes   rich colors
and made an after-sunset
mood   coffee on
a swinging bench
a tabby cat's tail
curled around my leg
I made images of time
how it was meant to be
spent   the sound
of slow waves
the sun deflating like
a balloon and
blowing up again
it's in the way
we breathe
and sip our pleasure
fruits we write
and paint and
sing and go
swimming
in the morning
before I came
here it's like
I didn't understand
color before

Papaver crassifolium

plants are made from a fine architecture
when the sea levels rose
        they were equipped
      fruits at the tip
      seed-shaped houses on towering
              stilts   home grew out
          curved upwards
          light-trapping windows
      ran vertical stripes
              the rooftop captured
                  sunlight
      pacific waters swirled
              around the base
          and receded again
                  no garages   no garages for a millennium
          home resembles a snail
              shell's interior
          light filters in
                  through fibrous
              molds filigree
          the skyline hard
                  changes entirely
              globes of light

"spontaneous   within foundation wall"
a bunch of california hippies
with purple hair
and sloppy leaves
Whatever I make my life in
do I trust it enough to hold
could I fit into a wall
feel my shoulders pressed
and be happy to have something
to brace against while
I grow
many happy heads
sun children
alcoves for kissing
beach hair
and sand
wind surfers humping over
waves hellos winking
from every corner
the taste of
freckled skin

ah! floridian caterpillar
  thick green   legs
     star-shaped head
   a baby nearby
    each leaf surface
      a long journey
       of silver threads hair
      on the terrain
       deep lines
      a palm reader's joy
     when you get
      to the flower
     a frightening beauty
       shreds of torn
        silk pointed hard
        like dried fruit

The shock of being bent
      seeing my friend's
          name   a city
    and also a friend a place
    and also a body
  she was a painter what would she
        think about the colors I've seen
    a handsome man in a nutmeg suit
          a curb painted school bus yellow
          a school group t-shirts and backpacks
              like neon faeries
          a pond's slick agate surface
          a woman in a black coat
              carrying a white plastic bag
                with her lunch inside
              my friend I can be certain ate
                  pansy flowers
                in garden salads with sweet
                    tomatoes & bell peppers
                      off the vine
                isn't it something   this tricolor comes
                    from payne county
                      and I'm in pain
                    thinking about all the things
                      she'll never see

Once I saw a tattooed yellow flower
    with a lion's face
       yawning
           it was marked
  by an ancient calligraphy
black lines fanned from the center
   pointing all directions from which
      it came at home in a North American
    rock garden
       had also seen the stone walls
     of China
     had also ridden the open seas
it makes me think did the gods claw
     on the tigers' stripes
     did they whip zebras with black
   who drew these sure lines on
a plant called pansy
  no weakling could endure
    having its mouth needle-
    inked

first the bulb is basket woven
a hanging cavity a swallow's nest
the fibers fine and strong
like matted hair out
shoot several green slender-pointed
blades some lilt to them
behind a consistent stem
thick as an ink pen
erupting into a five-lipped sun
each yellow ray lifting like a ruffled
feather two petals pressed down
chubby legs lifting from the trunk
two upward-reaching arms the face of the flower
the darkest stamen makes a tongue
no eyes no nose but a sense of dancing
friendly and afraid
Iris is a doll begging
for embrace
a starfish
an ember
She does not need
to be looked at
to know she's alive

Once
I saw a snap dragon
take a javelin
and throw it at the sun
yolk spilled out of the wound
onto the flower its lower lip
grew a red spot
like a bulls eye
for sun rays to fix on
This is how the flower
made itself the target
of the sun's affection
ingenuity & charm
delicate vines reach and
wrap around themselves
as when I hold my
own body
Imagine this a flower
that hisses as
it climbs closer
to you

in bed together
I examine your pleats
painted strokes yellow
a sealed mouth
a man in his dressing gown
holds an erotic secret
What fabric would my own body
wear in the era of Kings and Queens
A prince is a beautiful woman
with power
his body is clean-shaven
and perfumed with good air
his hands are softer than mine
my prince's face is softer than mine
he has no scars or bad breeding
He has the potential to be cruel
likes watching me work
because work's what my body knows
I lift and scrub things
I see my prince in bed
when the lights are out his cock hardens
against me quietly I wait
my beauty is nothing in light
but in the dark I'm warm
and lovable
I'm tired and strong and soft
from work my dreams
are alive
with water and flight
My mind allows me
to observe
very closely
a flower I
want to turn
into a man
to fuck
he is a prince
I am a pauper
he is a prince

the first leaf
  the first green arm
    when was it born?
     spun out of the fibers of history
       colliding with myth
         the garden was filled
           with perfect shapes
           and perfect humans
            tended to them
             Milton said Adam & Eve
             didn't have tools
               they tied the bounty
                back plants grew
                 and grew like
                  human hair
                  They were useless
                    gardeners
                 there was really nothing
                    to do until
                     Satan arrived

Papaver alaskanum

in the beginning
  there were a lot of left-
  over butterflies what to do?
their wings were stuck to
 tall grasses
        after a while they
  fused and this is how
certain flowers were made
    this is why the center
    of the poppy has many
        small antennas
      this is why the butterflies
      come back

I've never met so many happy
radicals in my life
they're all shooting the same
direction   rocketing
they're in   good humor
because they have
women to cook for them
all the books they
quote are from outer space
A booming booming bombast
only a spoonful of
chocolate mousse shuts
them up I'm happy they're
here a few know some
good lines of
poetry

Viola lanceolata

leaves make up a green fence
for viola to hide behind
her friends are of various sizes
the tallest sticks out   a thumb
warning the others when the cat's
stalking through   grass
children are preparing their inner-
tubes for the river   viola and
her friends giggle with excitement
the tigress is the color of sun
her tail another vocal being
we were undressing shrieks the smallest
of the bunch & the leaves shake
their snake rattles viola says let
every day be summer each river
in the region has a name
but in her mind the river needs
none when all her friends
already know which one
they'll gather by

satellite
        I smile because you have
these planets around you
        this doesn't happen every day
waving to the universe
            with all those funny dreams
        in your head why why why
        can't I have a star
                the satellite cries
                Eat your peas says the cosmos

Narcissus angustifolius

Hairy roots
I can relate to you
have you ever been told to trim your pussy?
in my country house
I grew fat and happy
I didn't feed a human soul
animals all around me
whiskers and fur and coats
each winter my chin grew a hair
but so did the horse and
so did the dog grow
winter mittens
and the cat
winter eye brows
and pantaloons

They needed a backhoe
   to dig you out lily
   largesse one long trumpeting horn
fringed with green sayings
   some kinder notes
   rise willowing the leaves
     of the willow trees
     some fine sanctity
   breath work in a singer's
       chest getting ready
     for an aria Is it
         spring? the birds
     think so
       or perhaps they
         are rested
         the parts fit
         together lily
         the seasons
           lock I keep
             thinking
         I'll find
           my way
         I'll find
           my way

the organizing principle behind four
heads is that if one goes wrong
there are 3 left over to rely
upon
I woke up today still
a woman   blaa
now I have to pretend
I'm meek and agreeable
all day long I have to smile
at people I don't like
if I had 4 heads lily
one could smile
and 3 could be
cranky for me
one could say
thanks and
three could say
a hex upon you all
with one head
I'm single minded
make me a poet
of the soul
or make me a stock broker
oh to have more heads
to tell all my sorry
jokes I look awful
today but one of my heads
has washed and combed
her hair
un deux trois quatre
one two three four

Viola lanceolata

Hey says viola how did
my head get down here?
I was found   by the sour lake
a murderer drove his boot
across my back   no respect
for the body of a young girl
my name is viola lanceolata L. &
I will make sure this gentleman
rots in hell

Viola!
Why are you still dancing?
they've just told us the
earth is dead
You bought a blue and
yellow gown
but no one told
you this is a
funeral
Hush   quit
your giggles your
slippers are
caressing the ground
all the movements
taught to you
exercising your one-
two-threes one-two-threes
three of you humming
music one of
you about to cry
no fun for viola
says viola pretending
to pout twirling
now she's put her
hair up like
a halo
the world
is ending! I
shout
I don't care!
she says and
I too can't help
but smile

Iris started in a strange shell
tell me what's inside the package
with a hair-line crack is it corn
is it edible   a flower or
    a tiny red apple
  If I was as strong as this long
green leaf painted-over ridged
  remarkable in length strong
    enough to stand erect
      green a perfect idea
        when I see it it's nearly
      as familiar as my mother's
       skin the first leaf
       I touched with my baby-
        hand making contact
      marking the sense
        of touch in my memory
          grasses of many textures
         some sharp enough to cut
        some soft enough to
          taste the roots of yes
         when I was young I
          put grass in my body
           I pulled the young shoots
           out and ate their
           water-ripe tips
            there was a faint
             squeak when I
              pulled the blade
              away from
              its roost

Iris tenuissima

in addition to flowers
iris grew two prominent
dragonfly wings I want to fly
her wish was never granted
but she attracted many
winged creatures and they
envied her stability and rootedness
the bees buzzed in her ear
we are overworked every
day our poor tired wings
a frenzy while you sit
in your tall green chair
watching the river
drift dragonflies
too had similar
complaints the
sky is dizzy w/
winged creatures
so many close
calls one with
a butterfly one
with a starving
bird Iris
flutters her poor
stuck wings
trying to lift
certain she'd
been born
wrong

Iris tenuissima

we are still purple enough
to remember our friendship
it was '99 we were
in our parents' connected yard
there was a citrus smell
coming from the yellow
lemon tree the wind
shook out seeds
and pollen birds
left their loose
feathers on the ground
our leaves were
easter green
our petals purple
as a winter sky
spring made us
all limp
with too much
rainwater the
color of our
tongues glistened
and melted
open

Jasminum officinale

When   a specimen is
        uncared for   a sadness
            happens   a furry grey
                takes over
                pills itself
                    to the page
                which snags
                    intricate things
                    still live
                and where there
                    was once
                        petals of a flower
                        now a long 5fingered
                            empty   hand
                                is all
                            that   remains

Contend
with this ugly orchid's
      message
 the grammar
  and spelling both
   how the plant is smeared
   to the page a distressed
      look   distressing
        roots shock out
              stunned arms
      bending wrists at odd
   angles large holes torn
      in the leaf's fabric
        the color of sick paint
could this be? Read today
   in the paper about the
        EPA getting lax
     about toxic orange dust
        coating cars in Ohio
       like snow people
       can't afford to leave
          rust and iron and cough cough
          little kids are ill the poet's
              job to describe ruin   cities once
              green turned to mud no one
             would choose these colors
               for their homes yet
              chemicals so hushed up beneath
                the sink are talking oil
                and gas are talking
                the poor are hearing it first
                and the mother of sick kids
                   says it's making it hard for me to be a mother
                       it's making it hard for me to
                     protect my kids

Narcissus tazetta

Narcissus your beginning
was beautiful but you became
a monster Escape!
Your yellow crowns
do not match the disaster
that has become your face
where are your eyes
your beauty has become
a mouth
noseless   a forehead
eternally growing
multiple tongues trying
to kiss your own
image
A chemical wonder
A man decides his
body is worth more
than his life—he won't stop
until every muscle
glistens
and winks back
at him
You are lovely
you are lovely
says the vaporous
water
Narcissus you
cannot see your own
death growing
flesh   toxic round
bulbs the bad
bark of a tree
an insect with
No shape but
an ability to Blend
horrific camouflage
Something happened
in your head
Narcissus
your wits have
been vacated
two heads joined
A crown on either
end
where a chin
should be

Blame yourself says
Poppy you've built
all these spikey nodes
created distance so no one'll
approach you've made
yourself an impossible
flower
growing only indoors
wreathed by safe rituals
rising at 4 bed by nine
staring out of your own
distance observing his
hair the shape of his hands
how his hips move
chewing silence
pressing your lips to
your teeth
fearing so much
what your legs say
Harm harm from
your own spike
Oh shut up poppy
if no one can
love me with
my spike how
is it je t'adore
you ?

It was winter
    the girls
were getting snowed on
    in the yard
    their father was pelting
    them with fastballs
    happy as could be
    a boy again a father
    of sons his girls
hidden beneath sleeping bag
    fabric any changes
    in their shapes lost
      under their sumo size
now they were just glad
    targets flaring and
      mean teeth like
    rabbits ok with
      being clumsy
    ok with their
    red noses
    and seeing
      through tears
    small mothers to
    each other accidental
    victors they shock
    him with one
    to the head
    he stumbles
      invisible
    blood pours
    out onto
    the snow
      they sneak
    up close
      a fake dead man
      he screams himself
    alive
      and they scatter
    like birds

Rosa gallica is it true
    you once belonged to a cult
  of soft beings who made more
  petals than you needed and small
thorns to dissuade overeager hands
  a declaration against
  chilled in the night air
    smelling of damascus
  and the old world
    the moon worn like
   a ring each leaf clipped
  out a perfect paper snowflake
    Ah I tell you my wants
     are as mighty as yours
   it's obvious that I'll never
    be your equal
      but each Spring
      I'll try

Rosa setigera
 if I grow into
  my twin bed a lone
creature warmed by
  water bottle flesh
    to save on heat
   and spare my empty dreams
    from filling with a lost
      man who will any day
            marry who he
   loves the sour breath of
        a room
          hangs from my clothes
        a lost-ness
        carrying each year
        a wadded tissue
          in a coat
        my friendship with
           time wears thin
        my lips grow less plump
            the quiet hour
             conspires to embrace
           my dying orchid
             with spring light
           I'm relieved from
             a trend in un imaginative
               thinking alone not
                  so bad when the world
                   lives with and
                     inside you

Rosa multiflora

content ment
a rose's maturity
spreads over years
A turtle in a pond
suns older than I am
New born birds take
risks hopping to an outer limb
farther than the day before
My feeling goes with
two grey haired
women walking at a brisk
pace wearing gentle fabrics
cataloging who's sick and
who's lucky to be alive
I put all my money
on friendship and love
a letter from my sister
includes what she hopes
to accomplish this year
she'd like to travel
to 1 new place
read a book a month
feel closer to her boyfriend
January sun I remove my scarf
and   bare my throat
to the elements
like a song bird I feel
my vocal chords
hum   I'm about
to start praising
everything I'm about
to praise everyone

dwarf iris sits
down in the forest theater
the woods are a curtain
of dripping leaves
the acoustics are as good
as any chapel
sunlight dims
small glowing specks
rush to the balcony
iris digs in her feet
pulls a covering
over her cold knees
the music begins
the air smells
like dirt and orange rind
the music takes on a shape
leaving the beginning
a few pinging droplets
then a steady rain
a crash occurs
startling everyone
the shadows
reveal two hunting

eyes a white
bolt snakes
across the sky
a powerful message
squeezes every last
thought there
is only sound
and shadows
sheets of water
obscure the dancers
on stage fighting over
ropes twisting their arms
and legs a final crack and
the sky breaks like a rubber
band someone cuts the water
it drips the dancers slow draping their
bodies across one another their white slippers
glow pointing upward the stars over the canopy return buffed
and glittering a washing sound moves over newly snapped reeds
beginning a steady hum the outlines of animals return to the stage
they have been fixed shadows now they move about smelling the cleaned air
night birds shake out their feathers then shrug into flight dipping low
from treetops like trapeze artists frogs build in a slow steady bass soil churns

Afterword

IN THE FALL OF 2017, I became a weekly visitor at the University of Texas's Plant Resources Center, the largest herbarium in the southwestern United States, holding over one million specimens from around the world.

Each week I signed the guest registry and, botanist and curator, Dr. George Yatskievych, helped me locate the flowers I was interested in viewing. We went floor to floor, wandering through aisles like library stacks. George opened metal cabinets, many seven feet high, and pulled out folders of *Lavandula vera*, *Lavandula angustifolia*, *Lavandula stoechas*, and, in the months to come, many other specimens that I could not pronounce the names of. My materials close at hand, I learned how to carefully move the legal-sized sheets of thick paper. Artistically, I had no idea what I was doing or what I was looking for. I simply sat down and tried to capture what I saw, hoping that the arrangement of the pressed plants on the page would influence my work. In a way, it felt like I was learning how to read—not words—but natural forms.

I worked at a small desk, isolated at the back of the building, with a window overlooking the turtle pond that was built as a memorial to the victims of the Tower shooting. With so many gun-related tragedies flaring up around the country it was haunting to sit in the chimney-like tower that had been the sniper's outpost on August 1, 1966, when he shot forty-three people, taking the lives of thirteen. In 2015, Gov. Greg Abbot gave licensed gun owners the right to carry concealed handguns onto UT's campus, signing into law S.B.11, better known as "campus carry." As a teaching assistant, I was nervous about the foreboding red signs that went up in classrooms about safety, the influx of interdepartmental emails regarding dealing with students displaying troubling behavior, and the routine "test" sirens that rang out across the sprawling forty-acre campus, causing all classroom lecturing or conversation to cease until the wailing alarm came to an end. Students and faculty took note of an increasingly heightened atmosphere of danger and fear. While I did not take part in protests, I felt a genuine sense of pride when students and faculty launched a campaign called "Cocks not Glocks." I smiled as I walked by young faces waving lolling dildos high in the air, distributing them free to passersby. Their point was astute: we live in a society more comfortable with violence than sex. Indeed, carrying a dildo on campus remains against university code.

As I worked at my small desk at the herbarium, I often looked up from my poems and watched students walk to class outside, as the seasons changed from fall to winter. I found myself (an agnostic) praying for their safety, wanting to protect each individual I saw with some sort of protective forcefield. I found it difficult not to think about Haruka Weiser, a UT freshman, who was raped and murdered on campus in 2016. Her body had been found in a creek bed by a bridge I walked over often. The university started a program called Sure Walk, which allowed students to request a volunteer to walk them home at night. Women were encouraged to walk in pairs after dark. I couldn't help but notice that the campus tours were thinning. The student tour guides had a harder time summing feel-good "Hook 'em horns" energy. The parents looked worried and potential students seemed less enthusiastic about whatever state of the art facilities and alluring amenities the university had to provide.

In the spring of 2017, at the very moment I was defending my master's thesis, a mentally ill student stabbed four other students outside of Gregory Gym. One of the victims died. The student who committed the crime had no memory of it. As someone with a mental illness, I understand how quickly our brains can distort reality. When I was a teenager, I took an overdose of my antipsychotic medication that caused me to hallucinate. I do not remember lunging toward my mother to strangle her, but the shame of knowing I attempted to harm her lives with me to this day.

My last semester, I was eager to graduate and leave UT's campus behind. That all changed when I took a wrong turn down a hallway. I had just dropped off my graduate thesis in a building called the Main Tower, or the Tower, a building I had no cause to visit until that moment, a building I passed every day because it is essentially the heart of the campus, a building I had no idea held the largest collection of plants from Texas in the world. I was used to looking up at the Tower's giant clock, the sound of the bell tower, the orange lights that would light up the façade on game nights but had never once, in the two years I'd been a student, been inside. I stood outside the windowless door with an old brass latch with a sign above it that read, "Press hard." I did, entering a room with low ceilings, florescent lights, and the distinct feeling of being hermetically sealed off from everything. Dr. George Yatskievych stepped out of his office and kindly offered me a tour. Before I left, I asked if it would be possible for a poet to stay to look at some specimens. He didn't see why not. He probably didn't know then—and I certainly didn't either—that I would hang around as the herbarium's unofficial poet-in-residence for close to three years.

After graduation, I could feel my life coming to a crossroads. In a month, I was slated to move to Orono, Maine to study poetics at the University of Maine. In a stagnate economy, with an unfit president, hopping from university to university seemed like the smart thing to do: I'd have an income from teaching, health insurance, and time to work on my book. Only something felt off; I didn't want to go.

At a coffee shop, I made a list of pros and cons, two columns: one for Austin and one for Orono. The pro list for Maine was much longer—I'd have the protection of a university for two years and get to live an affordable city with distinct seasonal changes. I called my mother, and she listened to me cry outside on the sidewalk, as a nearby freight train clattered past. She asked what I wanted to do. I nearly shouted that I want to stay in Austin and write about plants! I had to laugh at myself for turning down a fully-funded teaching assistantship but that's what I did later that day. A small miracle interceded on my behalf to help sway my decision: I won a nice purse as a finalist for the Keene prize, which meant I had options. I could stay clear of winter, get a part-time job at a bookstore, and write for a year—which is exactly what I did.

When I first began to write about the specimens, I thought my main interest was beauty. I even thought I might stumble upon the most beautiful plant in the herbarium, if not the world. The herbarium's holdings date back to the 1760s up to the present day. Gradually, I understood I wasn't interested in beauty at all, I was trying, in a sense, to heal myself from certain traumas I'd experienced in my life. The first time this thought occurred to me was when I was looking down at one particular plant; its branching stem was affixed to the page with small rectangular bits of cloth tape. The longer I looked the more I saw *limbs*—wrists, in fact, being held down. I flashed back to the spring of 2014 when I was hospitalized for bipolar disorder. Deemed a *flight risk*, I was held to a hospital bed in four-point restraint until I could be transported from the ER to the nearest psychiatric facility. I held in that position for many hours unable to move my arms and legs more than a few inches in any direction. As terrified as I was, I knew that to struggle would only make things worse. I did everything I could to keep an animalistic fear from rising up in my body. I saw myself mirrored in the plant resting on the table before me.

In the back of my mind, I always thought it was curious that I had chosen to spend time in the herbarium, located in the Tower, where I felt somehow located within a vortex of trauma. I could feel the many floors above me, a bit like being inside of tornado funnel, safe, but still at risk. Behind where I worked was the stairwell that George Whitman took to the observation deck, carrying with him two pistols, three rifles, and a sawed-off shotgun. Today, the stair-well remains locked at all times. Only staff members have a key, and a badge is required to operate the elevator. One day, I mistak-enly opened a door to the stairwell and trapped myself inside. My body felt paralyzed as I looked out the slender vertical window and knocked frantically. My legs shook as I remembered being locked in seclusion not knowing when the hospital staff would let me out. How quickly my brain manufactured a nightmare. How quickly my body remembered being flattened to the floor—arms, shoulders, legs pressed down until I felt a needle poked into my flesh. I tried not to think of these instances as violent because I had felt I had somehow done something to deserve it by being ill and "unman-ageable."

I didn't understand why I was suddenly remembering and, in a sense, physically reliving something that had happened to me three years previously. At that point, the therapy I'd received had been all but useless. I tried to remind myself that amidst turmoil and pain, there is always poetry. I was struck by the fact that George Whitman shared my favorite poet's last name. George, the name of my father, who passed away when I was eleven. And George also the name of the kind genius, who welcomed me into the herbarium. What be-gan as a meditation on beauty became a meditation on healing from violence. I spent hours looking at plants, I looked at them closely under a magnifier. I saw with my own eyes how closely plants mimic other patterns in life, in nature. The veins in a leaf like a network of streams, the veins in a transparent petal like the veins on the backs of my hands, the petal itself like my grandmother's soft papery skin. Then there was the aura I sensed of the sorts of lives the plants had lived—their connection with the landscape, the way the landscape shaped them, as my home had shaped me. In meditating on the flowers, getting to know their distinctive traits and characteristics, I felt a calmness spread through me like lava, I found a way to breathe again and release some of the anxieties caused by living in a modern world. I have no way of answering why violence persists. I have no way of knowing when or if the traumatization of being hospitalized will leave me. The only thing I'm certain of is this: observing nature up close has provided a path forward, a means of healing, a way to imagine what sort of world we could live in. In plant and animal forms, I believe there are lessons of peace and unity—these lessons are available to us to decipher if we are willing to observe. There were when times I thought this book might never find readers. I wrote these poems to sooth myself, to create a sort of lullaby I could return at night to reexperience the meditative state I felt while writing them. It is my greatest hope that readers might find a moment or two of comfort, it is my greatest hope that we embrace the fact that we are highly sensitive interconnected beings, rooted to the soil, branching across time, always and forever together.

Acknowledgments

To the amazing crew at Deep Vellum. My deepest gratitude to Will Evans for welcoming me into the DV family and for making my dream of publishing a *Green* book a reality. To *Borderlands: Texas Poetry Review* for publishing "Nymphaea mexicana," the *Texas Observer* for publishing "Iris tenuissima" in their culture newsletter; *Oddball Magazine* for publishing "Lavandula Vera;" *Denver Quarterly* for publishing "Iris tenuissima," "Rosa rugosa," and "Lilium michauxii;" and *Poet Lore* for publishing "Iris tenuissima" and "Iris missouriensis." To the brilliant eyeballs of Taisia Kitaiskaia, Katelin Kelly, Austin Rodenbiker, and Stephaine Goehring. To Aileen Morrow for the beautiful cover. To Chory Ferguson, my partner in literary crime. To my Columbia University mentors Josh Bell, Jeffrey Greene, and Priscilla Becker. To my University of Texas at Austin New Writers Project mentors Dean Young and Noelle Kocot. To Path with Art and Hugo House for encouragement just when I thought I might never be able to write again. To the University of Texas Keene Prize committee for selecting me as a finalist, making it possible for me to stay in Austin and write about plants. To the Helene Wurlitzer Foundation and Yaddo for enabling me to take myself seriously as a poet. To Malvern Books for being a second home. To my friends, you know who you are. To my family, you know who you are. To Dr. George Yatskievych, curator of the Billie L. Turner Plant Resources Center at the University of Texas at Austin, this book would not have been possible without your generosity and kindness—thanks for letting me become the herbarium's unofficial poet-in-residence. To the specimens for making me think, feel, laugh, cry, and wonder-up different possibilities for how to see the world. To my friend Chaya Grace Stillwater-Lanz, who I will never forget, in friendship, in loving memory.

JULIE POOLE was born and raised in the Pacific Northwest. She has received scholarships and fellowship support from the James A. Michener Center, the Helene Wurlitzer Foundation, and Yaddo. In 2017, she was a finalist for the Keene Prize for Literature. Her poems and essays have appeared in *Cold Mountain Review*, *CutBank*, *Poet Lore*, *Denver Quarterly*, and elsewhere. She lives in Austin, Texas, with her growing collection of found butterflies.

PARTNERS

pixel texel

ADDITIONAL DONORS, CONT'D

Mark Haber
Mary Cline
Maynard Thomson
Michael Reklis
Mike Soto
Mokhtar Ramadan
Nikki & Dennis Gibson
Patrick Kukucka
Patrick Kutcher
Rev. Elizabeth & Neil Moseley
Richard Meyer

Scott & Katy Nimmons
Sherry Perry
Sydneyann Binion
Stephen Harding
Stephen Williamson
Susan Carp
Susan Ernst
Theater Jones
Tim Perttula
Tony Thomson

SUBSCRIBERS

Joseph Rebella
Michael Lighty
Shelby Vincent
Margaret Terwey
Ben Fountain

AVAILABLE NOW FROM DEEP VELLUM

MICHÈLE AUDIN · *One Hundred Twenty-One Days*
translated by Christiana Hills · FRANCE

BAE SUAH · *Recitation*
translated by Deborah Smith · SOUTH KOREA

MARIO BELLATIN · *Mrs. Murakami's Garden*
translated by Heather Cleary · MEXICO

EDUARDO BERTI · *The Imagined Land*
translated by Charlotte Coombe · ARGENTINA

CARMEN BOULLOSA · *Texas: The Great Theft* · *Before* · *Heavens on Earth*
translated by Samantha Schnee · Peter Bush · Shelby Vincent · MEXICO

LEILA S. CHUDORI · *Home*
translated by John H. McGlynn · INDONESIA

SARAH CLEAVE, ed. · *Banthology: Stories from Banned Nations* ·
IRAN, IRAQ, LIBYA, SOMALIA, SUDAN, SYRIA & YEMEN

ANANDA DEVI · *Eve Out of Her Ruins*
translated by Jeffrey Zuckerman · MAURITIUS

ROSS FARRAR · *Ross Sings Cheree & the Animated Dark: Poems* · USA

ALISA GANIEVA · *Bride and Groom* · *The Mountain and the Wall*
translated by Carol Apollonio · RUSSIA

ANNE GARRÉTA · *Sphinx* · *Not One Day*
translated by Emma Ramadan · FRANCE

JÓN GNARR · *The Indian* · *The Pirate* · *The Outlaw*
translated by Lytton Smith · ICELAND

GOETHE · *The Golden Goblet: Selected Poems* · *Faust, Part One*
translated by Zsuzsanna Ozsváth and Frederick Turner · GERMANY

NOEMI JAFFE · *What are the Blind Men Dreaming?*
translated by Julia Sanches & Ellen Elias-Bursac · BRAZIL

CLAUDIA SALAZAR JIMÉNEZ · *Blood of the Dawn*
translated by Elizabeth Bryer · PERU

JUNG YOUNG MOON · *Seven Samurai Swept Away in a River* · *Vaseline Buddha*
translated by Yewon Jung · SOUTH KOREA

KIM YIDEUM · *Blood Sisters*
translated by Ji yoon Lee · SOUTH KOREA

JOSEFINE KLOUGART · *Of Darkness*
translated by Martin Aitken · DENMARK

YANICK LAHENS · *Moonbath*
translated by Emily Gogolak · HAITI

FOUAD LAROUI · *The Curious Case of Dassoukine's Trousers*
translated by Emma Ramadan · MOROCCO

FORTHCOMING FROM DEEP VELLUM

MAGDA CARNECI · *FEM*
translated by Sean Cotter · ROMANIA

MIRCEA CĂRTĂRESCU · *Solenoid*
translated by Sean Cotter · ROMANIA

MATHILDE CLARK · *Lone Star*
translated by Martin Aitken · DENMARK

LOGEN CURE · *Welcome to Midland: Poems* · USA

PETER DIMOCK · *Daybook from Sheep Meadow* · USA

CLAUDIA ULLOA DONOSO · *Little Bird*, translated by Lily Meyer · PERU/NORWAY

LEYLÂ ERBIL · *A Strange Woman*
translated by Nermin Menemencioğlu · TURKEY

FERNANDA GARCIA LAU · *Out of the Cage*
translated by Will Vanderhyden · ARGENTINA

ANNE GARRÉTA · *In/concrete*
translated by Emma Ramadan · FRANCE

JUNG YOUNG MOON · *Arriving in a Thick Fog*
translated by Mah Eunji and Jeffrey Karvonen · SOUTH KOREA

FISTON MWANZA MUJILA · *The Villain's Dance*, translated by Roland Glasser · *The River in the Belly: Selected Poems*, translated by Bret Maney · DEMOCRATIC REPUBLIC OF CONGO

LUDMILLA PETRUSHEVSKAYA · *Kidnapped: A Crime Story*, translated by Marian Schwartz · *The New Adventures of Helen: Magical Tales*, translated by Jane Bugaeva · RUSSIA

MANON STEFAN ROS · *The Blue Book of Nebo* · WALES

ETHAN RUTHERFORD · *Farthest South & Other Stories* · USA

BOB TRAMMELL · *The Origins of the Avant-Garde in Dallas & Other Stories* · USA